Balboa Press books may be ordered through booksellers or by contacting:

Balboa Press
A Division of Hay House
1663 Liberty Drive
Bloomington, IN 47403
www.balboapress.com
844-682-1282

Interior Image Credit: Cindy Monten

ISBN: 979-8-7652-3569-0 (sc)
ISBN: 979-8-7652-3570-6 (e)

Library of Congress Control Number: 2022919182

Print information available on the last page.

Balboa Press rev. date: 01/18/2023

BALBOA.PRESS

The Birth of Wonderment

Dedicated to:
Zoë August Monten
I am grateful daily to be your mom.
You are my sparkle and I love you as big as the moon.
I am in your heart and you are also in mine,
From the moment you were conceived until the end of time.

Bert Monten
For loving me as no one had ever loved me before
You were my champion. You live in my heart always

Special thanks to: Cuky Choquette Harvey
Thank you for being my guide on my Lomi-Lomi journey.
You helped me to reclaim my spirit and embrace myself

Cheryl Cowie

For loving assistance with edits

My Spirit Family

You all know who you are, some my biological family, others who are my chosen tribe, my dearest friends. Those who know everything about me and honor me with your love. You believe in me & helped me rekindle my light when I thought it was gone forever.

I shine bright, illuminated by your love.

Thank you for loving me through it all and encouraging me to live a creative life and be true to that which I am.

Forward

This is a true story, although parts of it read like a fairytale.

The autumn of 2008 was an ugly, very dark and difficult time, in my life.

I think I had been slipping for a long time but did not recognize it. I had always been the tough little cookie, powering through everything life tossed my way. My way of dealing was to put more on my plate and I kept adding and adding and never really stopped to look deeply into my own heart and acknowledge what I really needed to be happy. I had never asked myself the three important questions.

Who am I? What do I want? What is my purpose?

Essentially, I was not living my life. Instead, I was wandering in a fog, struggling to meet expectations that I perceived had been placed on me by other people. The reality is that when we do this to ourselves, eventually we run out of gas.

CHAPTER 1

This chapter is not to paint myself as a victim, because I am not. I do feel it is important to give some background. It is to serve as a comparison, so that you will understand what a profound shift getting to "Wonderment" has been and to give you hope that you can get there too. My life has been a series of sudden beginnings and sudden endings.

It seems I had just gotten used to the roller coaster drama and considered it normal. I even created some of the drama myself, because it seemed so normal. If I did not create it, then I most certainly attracted circumstances and people into my world that created chaos.

I know that seems really silly. Why would someone do that to themselves? I do believe we create and attract what feels comfortable to us. As crazy as it sounds, I know in my own life that was true.

Certainly I cannot say that I am 100% responsible for everything that has gone awry in my life. Sometimes life or stuff just happens!

However, I do believe that everything is energy and like attracts like. When we are in balance and our energy is positive, we attract more positivity, abundance and blessings.

If our energy is depleted or unbalanced, we draw negativity into our energy field and this translates to lack, betrayal, dysfunction and suffering.

We stop allowing other people to take advantage of us when we learn the art of self-love and self-care. We can then take action and do what it takes for us to become balanced. Then, we attract people and situations that are also in balance and joyful. In this type of energy, life tends to flow along in a much happier way.

When we are out of balance and thus attracting negative energy, our lives and relationships can be like swimming upstream in mud, while dodging large rocks in the process.

I believe that some of our energy is inherited from past lives or handed down to us at both a cellular level and at a spiritual level through the energy of our parents or other ancestors.

I have drawn on my own personal experience and do not profess to be an expert in this area. There are experts in this type of thinking and you will find a list of suggested reading later on.

Not sleeping for more than a few hours a night and feeling angry, frustrated, irritable and moody (even with those you love more than anything), is not normal and certainly not healthy.

It is not normal or healthy to be unable to think clearly and be so forgetful that you lose your keys and/or your phone several times every day. Seriously, there was a while there when the receptionist in the salon I owned at the time would make finding my keys, my phone or something else a daily task.

The symptoms I mention are the signs of someone who is under a great deal of stress. Medical research shows that prolonged stress can cause adrenal burnout. These symptoms can also be considered signs of depression.

For me, it took several months to discover that these may also be signs of a serious hormone imbalance. In my case a combination of events led me to go into "Tilt" mode.

A dear friend told me that she thought I had finally had the breakdown I should have had years before when my husband lost his battle with cancer, leaving me to raise our four year old daughter -alone. I believe it all started years before when I was just a child myself.

Babies were not planned then and I certainly was not. I was a third child born to a young couple who had little money or education.

My oldest sister Debbie and I were not close as children. It seems that we were always at odds and by the time I was 13 she had moved out of the house. It was not until many years later that I realized she had spent years trying to protect us from the reality of my father's drinking and could not take it anymore.

My second sibling Babs, is developmentally disabled. We are less than 2 years apart. She did not walk until she was two and did not talk until she was almost 4.

Babs needed much more care and attention than I did and I do not begrudge her that. I was the spunky, resourceful one -so everyone assumed I was fine. Because of this, I was often overlooked and left to my own devices. My youngest sister Jennifer came along when I was just two; she was everyone's favorite, including mine.

I always felt responsible for both she and Babs. This was not pressure anyone put on me, it was something I did to myself.

Early on I ended up babysitting and cooking for both Babs & Jennifer as my mom worked a lot. I do not recall my dad working after I was about 12. He drank and his health deteriorated.

Eventually, that wore me down too and I moved out of my parent's home the first time when I was 15 and permanently when I was 17.

The short version is that it was a dysfunctional childhood. No better or worse than many other kids. Not horribly abused, but overlooked by parents with too much responsibility for their skill set. I guess like so many families we did our best with our then current level of consciousness, intellect and financial resources. The truth is our best was not very good and seemed to get worse as the years went by.

One thing I believe is that every child deserves to be taught how to love themselves. Children need to have their value confirmed by the adults in their life, to develop healthy self -esteem. Self-esteem is the greatest gift a parent can give a child.

It took me so many years and so many tears to realize that this had been a missing link in my childhood.

I was simply overlooked and because of this spent a lot of time seeking the approval of others, instead of listening to my own spirit.

When we do this, it clouds our ability to tap into our inner wisdom. This leads to bad choices and we create more drama for ourselves.

*"You, yourself, as much as anybody in the entire universe,
deserve your love and affection."
- Buddha*

About a year after I had fallen apart completely, a friend told me about Cuky Harvey and her work as a Lomi-Lomi master.

It is my understanding that, Lomi-Lomi is an ancient form of Hawaiian bodywork that can help to facilitate deep healing.

Ancient Hawaiians believed it can call your true spirit home. For me it was a transformational journey.

In the spring of 2010 I did what is called a 3 day Lomi-Lomi Journey.

I spent several hours each day receiving sessions with, Lomi-Lomi Master, Cuky Choquette Harvey. In this book, I refer to Cuky as my guide.

Each day when we were finished, she encouraged me to take some time to capture what had happened for me during our time together. She told me that this type of deep bodywork can open emotional blocks so I should pay attention to whatever came up and write it down.

I was shocked by the vivid images and descriptive words that poured from me after our first session together. I took my journal and sketch pad to a park and the information just flowed onto the pages.

I had never written anything like this, nor had I ever drawn like this. Quickly and effortlessly, the story arrived. I journaled and illustrated my thoughts and images. I have always thought in pictures - as many creative and sensitive people do. I had not really ever tried to draw what I saw in my mind.

At the end of day 3, I realized that what had begun as my personal journal -must become a little book.

It is a story of rebirth, reconnecting with myself, a story of hope.

It was like stepping into the sun.

That book has lived in the pages of my journal. Now I choose to share it, because it is a story of hope, healing, and of how powerful we become -when we realize that our best days come when we lovingly embrace our true self.

It is a story of my painful history, and profound changes.

This kind of change only happens when we put our ego aside, peel back the layers and look deeply at ourselves and how we came to be where we are in this moment. Then, the past can become the past and the future becomes amazing, brighter, more beautiful and more powerfully filled with possibility than we could ever imagine.

The images in this book have been inspired by my original sketches. The originals were done in merely minutes and flowed from me as easily as the words I have written here. As though tapping into myself, calling my spirit home unleashed a new set of gifts and talents I had no idea that I possessed.

I think the originals are most honest because they were born of raw emotion. I redrew them to add color and make them easier to view, as the originals were too small to photograph well.

Before I get into the details of the Lomi-Lomi Journey I need to give you a little bit of the back-story.

Be mindful of your health. If you do not sleep well, find out why. Take time each day to quiet your mind and listen to your spirit.

Make time to meet your own needs before meeting the needs of everyone else. This is not to say, be selfish, just put on your own oxygen mask first, (especially if you are highly sensitive as I am).

We cannot bring our best self to the world if we do not take care to become our best self.

If anyone had ever told me that in the fall of 2008 my life would resemble an egg that had been tossed at a concrete wall, I would have thought they had lost their minds.

Yet, that is what happened. I fell apart completely- like a broken windup toy that had lost her key. I could not function! I lay on the floor and cried and cried and cried. I had no idea one could manage so many tears. I lost 35 pounds in about 20 days.

I was just completely spent, physically, emotionally, spiritually, energetically and financially.

I sold a home I loved, walked away from a business that had once been my dream and passion, failed many people I cared for deeply and the worst of it was, I moved my daughter out of the house a few months prior to her 16th birthday. I sent her to live with relatives because I could not even take care of myself, much less her. I did not want her to see me this way, I know she was frightened, not of me, but for me. I was not the mother she knew and wise though she was, she was a child and did not know how to help.

Once a very "in control", and some would say controlling woman, now I could not make a decision to save my life. I did not eat, could not sleep and my hair was falling out. My friends and family no longer recognized me. I no longer recognized myself. I pushed everyone away and isolated myself.

I was misdiagnosed and mistreated for depression with medications that only made things worse.

It was on a day that my daughter came to visit me in the temporary condo I had rented after selling our home that I knew something had to change.

My mother had often been so depressed she could not have a conversation. I had become her.

My daughter laid on the couch with her head in my lap and with tears in her eyes said, "Mama, you promised me you would never be like this, like Grandma Elaine. Please mom, come back"

My already broken heart shattered into a million pieces like shards of mirrored glass and I could almost feel myself begin to bleed internally. It was in that moment I realized that I must take action I had to find a way to fix this.

I had to get better. I am her only parent; her father had died of cancer when she was just 4 years old.

My voice broke when I spoke and promised I would figure it out.

I went to see my doctor. After waiting for 90 minutes after my appointed time, I was finally escorted into his office. I told him I felt worse than I ever had before. The medication made my sweat smell like a toxic waste dump and I was bathed in sweat all the time. My hair was falling out, even though he tried to convince me otherwise. When I said I could not sleep, he suggested that he give me yet another prescription to help me sleep.

"Are you kidding me? " I then asked if it could be hormonal and his response was "No, of course not."

Well, I disagreed and told him he was fired and to send my medical records to me. I promptly went home and flushed my medications down the toilet. I had to regain my life.

I am not suggesting that anyone else do this. I do think that for some people medication is critical and every situation is different.

However, I just knew he was wrong in my case. I searched the internet for articles on vitamin deficiencies and depression. I found some good information and immediately began taking high doses of vitamin B-complex, D3 and magnesium. My boyfriend at the time had given me a little mood light that was supposed to simulate daylight, but it did not help much.

I went to a tanning booth to help activate the D3, because I had read somewhere that it helped.

It did help a little, but not enough -so I continued my research.

I began looking at hormone imbalance. I read several books and articles that described my symptoms and what I was dealing with. There is a lot more to it than hot flashes!

There are mood swings, anger, foggy thinking, indecision, and insomnia. The The lack of cognitive thinking and an inability to make good decisions had been getting worse over the course of a couple of years. I thought it was just stress.

I had a consultation with a Bio Identical Hormone specialist. He prescribed a balanced combination of bio identical hormone replacement therapy that was customized for my body. Within three days, I slept through the night for the first time in years. The world was a different color when I woke that morning, everything looked brighter.

I recall thinking to myself, "Oh, so this is what it feels like to be rested, I feel fabulous!"

I called him to report that I was amazed and grateful. He laughed and told me

"If you feel good now, just wait 6 months."

The scary thing is what could have happened if I had not found this information and this doctor. What if I had not met a really good therapist? It made me wonder about the women in earlier years that had gone undiagnosed or misdiagnosed. I wonder how many women I know have experienced the same thing?

My mother is deceased but after discussing her medical history with my doctor, I am certain that it was a hormone imbalance that led to her early death. Remember, I am not a medical professional and this is only my personal story. There is a lot of research that points to hormone imbalances as a catalyst for diabetes and heart disease.

There are many opinions from many sources out there on the topic. To debate this is not the purpose of this book.

This information is to give you a bit of the back-story to create perspective for you as you read the story of "Wonderment"

I worked hard to peel back the layers and heal from all of this. I did work with a psychologist as well, to take a closer look at how I had been affected by childhood traumas and how all of that played a role in my current reality.

I had been concerned about my daughter, and how the impact of all we have been through has affected her. This is why I decided to follow the advice of my friend and made a phone call to Hawaiian healing Arts Specialist, Cuky Harvey, as the next step in my healing.

My concern for my daughter had been the catalyst for this journey. It had been 18 months since I fell apart and I was feeling much better -but felt called to dig deeper.

I reserved a 3 day Lomi-Lomi Journey for both Zoë & I.

We would each have one healing session each day for three consecutive days. Each session would be a few hours long.

Zoë & I traveled to Kansas from Minnesota to work with Cuky so it was a commitment of both time and money to do this.

I also want to say that every Lomi-Lomi Journey is different and very personal. Zoë had her own experience and it is personal, so I will not be discussing that.

I do know that regardless of where you are on your life path, Lomi-Lomi may help you feel better and more connected to yourself.

This story has been inside me a long time. It is my spirit story. I had done some other types of healing work. I worked with a counselor who helped me as well, she gave me the courage to dig deeper. In fact, I had planned to do more work with her. When I returned from my journey and read her the story, her response was, "Girl you've got this, you do not need me anymore!"

It is my belief that my experience was so profound because I had so much healing to do and also because I was just so ready to shift. This allowed me to open my heart and get in touch with myself enough to write and illustrate the story.

Part of my journey in this life is to share this information, to be the storyteller. I am telling the story to further, not only my own healing but that of others as well.

While it is a story of falling apart, it is also a story of taking off your armor, laying down your fear-based ego and opening your heart.

Wonderment is a story of finding out who you are, and being true to that.

To lift the veil, remove emotional blocks, connect to your spirit and call it home.

When I think about this, it reminds me of the part in the children's story "Peter Pan", where Peter loses his shadow and Wendy sews it back on for him. Only in this case, our spirit is not our shadow that we have lost, it is our light that we must sew back on!

Finding your spirit is like turning on your light, so you can see your true gifts and talents. It empowers you to be your most authentic self.

Your spirit light is the beacon that draws positivity to you like a magnetic current.

We all have a story to tell, we all have unique treasures to share.

Many of us are wounded and do not even know that we are.

Yet these wounds manifest in our lives as drama, suffering and broken relationships.

Those who have been wounded can make great healers, because they really know what being wounded feels like.

From my heart with all my love

Here is the story of my Lomi-Lomi journey.

My hope is that it will encourage you to find your own story, your own voice and your own path to healing.

CHAPTER 2

Day 1 The Journey Begins

Lomi-Lomi
Day 1

I am looking forward to this day because I know that Lomi-Lomi is a type of bodywork. I love to be touched, and I am weary after the events of the last year and half. It has been a traumatic time mentally, physically and emotionally. My heart and my spirit have been broken and I am seeking recovery. I want out of "Stuckville" - the self-imposed dysfunctional place I have lived in my heart.

Zoë and I had flown to Kansas for a three day Lomi-Lomi journey, scheduled with Hawaiian Healing Arts Specialist - Cuky Harvey.

We decided that Cuky would work with me in the morning and Zoë in the afternoon. Teenagers like to sleep in and I have always been a morning person, so this plan was perfect.

We would each have a session each day, for the next 3 days.

I arrived on her doorstep at the appointed time on the first day.

From the moment Cuky opened the door, I knew I was exactly where

I was supposed to be and that this would be a very special day.

She directed me to the room where we would be working and gave me a brief explanation of what the practice of Lomi-Lomi is. She told me that it can create a shift and bring up some deep feelings and I should be prepared for that.

She explained that our body is like an island, like a sleeping goddess and Lomi-Lomi helps to awaken us to whom we are, to our true spirit.

She also encouraged me to capture my thoughts and feelings from each session, with either a journal or drawing.

I did both and the result is this book- "The Birth of Wonderment".

I lay on the massage table, and as Cuky began her work - I almost instantly slipped into a very deep, almost dreamlike state. It became like watching a movie, only I was playing lead. A bit of an out of body experience, I was aware of my body, but did not feel connected to it.

As I watched this "movie" play in my mind the first image was me laying on my belly with a dysfunctional city on my back. I was trying to reach up to get out from under it. The pages that follow are how this story played out.

Day 1

The City of Pain

Lioness Mother

Today the goddess within me awakened. Many, many years she had lain dormant, crushed under the weight of the "City of Pain "that I had carried so long upon my back. A city filled with grief, regret, dysfunction, sacrifice, pain, suffering, and deceit. A city largely of my own making, a city I have come to think of as, "Stuckville."

This city was filled with toxic people, places, and things that no longer serve me. A city I had been trying to pull my creative soul out from under, but instead had succeeded only in making it worse.

The volcano erupts, spewing molten oxblood red and inky black lava. It storms down the mountains of my shoulders and streams in thick burning rivers down my back, over my hips, pouring down my arms and falls off my hands and feet, into the turquoise waters that surround the island that I Am.

This tsunami of lava crushes and burns the entire "City of Pain" and all of the evil living within it.

The lava has become so heavily laden with the debris, it crashes to the bottom of the ocean floor and rushes into cool dark caves. An underwater earthquake ensues, causing huge chunks of rock and coral to break free then tumble and roll into the mouths of these caves, sealing the ashes of the "City of Pain" within - forever more! No more harm will come from it.

The ocean bubbles and boils and hisses with steam, sighing as if to say, "It is over, it is over Wonderment. Now you are free!"

I have been washed clean of the burden of it all. The clean lava that remains cools and dries, fusing my bones together with a strength that can never be broken. Every bone, no matter how large or small, is now coated in bedrock that dries miraculously smooth, white and clean, like an elephants tusk.

The storm has passed, my spirit animal, (my lioness mother) pads softly to me. Her huge paws mark her path, but her approach is silent. Her powerful muscles ripple under her caramel colored fur, her liquid amber eyes, gaze upon me filled with love.

My flesh reappears over my new-old bones, soft and smooth as a newborn, but covered yet, with just a bit of volcanic dust.

She settles beside me and gently begins the task of bathing me with her tongue, as though I am her newborn cub.

Her tongue is warm and wet, the texture of fine sandpaper. She gently and firmly licks me clean until I sparkle and shine, damp and glistening in the sunlight, breaking through the clouds.

I sigh.........deeply peaceful and content as I roll onto my back, the sunlight warm, orange, sweet and delicious makes me glow from the inside out.

The sunlight shifts and a shadow falls grey and cool, across my belly.

As I blink into the light my eyes look into my eyes. Hers are the exact shade of green, the shape identical and are a mirror image of my own.

My goddess mother stands over me and lifts me gently into her arms and snuggles me, my belly against her breast, cheek to cheek, skin to skin.

She lifts me and tips me away from her, as she pushes the hair from my face and gazing into my eyes with love, she speaks to me in a voice as warm and sweet as amber honey.

"Welcome my darling child; this is the birth that I had planned for you. I am so sorry that it has taken so long for you to arrive and that your past journeys have been so painful."

"I am with you now and Wonderment is your name."

"It is time for you to claim all the gifts of the universe that are your birthright. Your father and I shared great love in your creation and that great love and peace live within you and are yours to share with the world"

"Listen my child, do you hear the warm waves washing on shore, and do you feel the breeze gently blowing all the fragrance of flowers and spice from the tropical gardens your way?"

The scents of vanilla, cinnamon, cardamom, frangipani, jasmine, coffee and coconut fill my nostrils and my mouth begins to water with anticipation of beauty, not yet revealed.

"It is the wind of change and sweet new beginnings for you, Wonderment. Turn your face into the wind with no fear, breathe it in", her honeyed voice advises me.

She set me on my feet and reached out her hand to me and said, "Come".

In one hand she held a fragrant broom made of sage, lemongrass, soft pine boughs, bay leaves and palm fronds.

My goddess mothers broom swept the rocks and gravel from the path that had suddenly appeared before us.

With each brush the weeds and debris that had littered the path disappeared and were replaced with pristine white sand, packed hard to allow a smooth place to walk.

We stepped forward together and the path became covered with multicolored fragrant flower petals the sweet aromas rising to meet us as the petals crushed under our feet.

The edge of the path was lined with a mosaic of precious stones, of every kind. There were diamonds, rubies, rich blue sapphires, peridots that were the color of new grass in spring, warm yellow citrine and emeralds as green as the forest. The border of the mosaic was made of piles and piles of gold coins, stacked to form a casual border to our flower and gem path.

She held my hand and brushed as we walked. The path continued to develop with our steps, flowers, precious gems and gold coins. Again she spoke in her honeyed voice, sharing her wisdom with me.

"It does not matter which way you go my dear Wonderment, this is what your path will look like from now on. It is so and so it shall be. Your heart knows this to be the truth"

Then she turned to me and again my eyes looked into the eyes that were a mirror of mine. She laid her hand on my heart. "Your heart is a prism and you are golden light. All the colors of the rainbow stream from your heart, throwing lovely dancing colors before you lighting your path and blessing all those whose lives you touch. You must be heart centered in all you do."

She continued with her hand still warm and soft on my heart

"Have no fear, your Father the King has his hand on your back, and you will not falter. Be true to your creative spirit and quiet your mind.

Your hands are your paintbrush, your canvas anything you wish."

"Be still," she said gently. "There is nothing more to say, I will be right here beside you. Archangels Michael and Gabriel also walk beside you. Use your gifts, embrace your creativity, and do not try to be that which you are not. Embrace your creativity and all will be well'. Her words melted into my skin like butter on warm bread, seeping into every pore.

"You are a slave no longer, you are free. Be true to the goddess within, she slumbers no more. Welcome her home, Wonderment. She is you, love her well."

"All the love, peace, and abundance of the universe are yours; you need only to accept them. Allow them to come to you to make them yours. They are your birthright as the goddess "Wonderment".

It is so and so it shall be."

I know in my deepest awareness that she speaks the truth. I have worn heavy armor of fear, shame, insecurity and guilt. I have masked it by wearing the feathers of a peacock, but that is not who I am.

It is this armor weighing heavily on my heart that has blocked the love I crave so much.

At the end of day 1, I was instructed to take my time getting up from the massage table. I lay on the massage table and cried for what seemed like a very long time. When I finally emerged Cuky was there waiting with some water. I took one look at her and burst into tears again and hugged her with all my might!

They were not tears of sorrow but tears of relief -to lay my burden down. I knew

I was in the hands of a healer.

CHAPTER 3

Day 2 The Journey Continues

Day 2

The Mountain of the Grandmothers

My Father the King & Goddess Mother

Today I awake very early, the intention is to go to the gym for a good workout.

My weary body disagrees and begs for more sleep.

My brain finally listens and I drift back to sleep for an additional 3 hours. This time when I wake I am refreshed and excited for my day of Lomi-Lomi and my visit with my guide.

The Mountain of the Grandmothers

I begin at the far end of the island that is me, near the tidal pools. My guide urges me to travel along the edge of the island where I can look down at the turquoise waters below as I climb toward the lower mountain known as, "The Mountain of

The Grandmothers".

My senses are heightened and I can feel the hair on the back of my neck flutter in anticipation with every breeze that ripples in soft waves against my skin.

The moist earth, mixed with the clean smell of sunshine and ocean salt is layered with the sensuous aroma of ripe tropical fruits and exotic flowers. The effect on me is intoxicating and welcomes my soul like an invisible ribbon of love pulling me forward.

When I arrive at the gates of the mountain, the Grandmothers stand guard shoulder to shoulder, blocking my path and preventing me from traveling onward.

The eldest steps forward and stops me with one finger placed firmly on my chest. Her wise eyes look directly into mine and in a very crisp, firm but not unkind

voice, she asks, "Who are you and what do you want?"

"Grandmother," I reply, "Do you not remember me? I am Wonderment and I have come home. I have been gone a very long time and I have endured many painful journeys, but this is where I belong. I am the Goddess of the Island and she is me".

"A-h-h." she breathes softly, "Indeed you are, our Wonderment! Indeed, you have come home to us. We have never forgotten you, even when your heart forgot us, and you left your spirit behind.

We know why you are here; we just want to be certain that you know."

Her wise eyes are a mirror image of my own eyes. They are the same soft fern green as my own, dancing with joy and laughter and the lines in her face tell me the stories of my ancestors, back, back to the dawn of time.

The others join in the laughter as they surround me and take turns passing me around the circle, so that I can hold their hands and hug and kiss each one as they welcome me home, to the Goddess Island that is me.

They anoint me with exotic scented oils after they bathe me under the waterfall and tie flowers in my hair.

Each one adds a large precious stone to the necklace that they now place around my neck.

The necklace is heavy but not unpleasant. The sun dances across the rare gems making them shine, iridescent in the light. The eldest then takes my hand and leads me back to the path that continues up the mountain.

"It is time," she gently instructs as she nudges me forward.

"Your Father, the King is anxious for your arrival."

My Father, The King

I move swiftly and deftly as a mountain goat up the lush incline. Moving closer to the highest peak of what I now consider my mountain. My Father's love and spirit silently call me to his side.

The path becomes steeper as I traverse back and forth. At last, I am momentarily shrouded in the mist of clouds, before stepping on to the smooth solid alter at the top of the highest peak.

Here, my Father the King, waits for me. His skin is as smooth as toffee colored marble. His beautiful mouth opens in laughter and his eyes crinkle in merriment. His laughter rolls like thunder and washes over me in great waves.

He scoops me up with one massive hand and cups my face with the other. "Wonderment, my darling girl, you have come home! This pleases me a great deal."

I am suddenly a small child and naked before him except for the gift of the

Grandmothers' necklace, and yet I feel no shame.

His strong jaw and broad shoulders make me feel as small as an acorn in his hands.

He continues speaking in a deep baritone that makes me want to snuggle in closer to each word.

"Wonderment, my child - you have been lost but now you have found your way home to us and to your own heart."

He sweeps his hand across the vista and indicates the breath taking view of the ocean and the lush valley below.

"This is your home, this is all yours. The Island of the Goddess is yours and you are hers."

He sets me on my feet and suddenly I am a child no more. He slips a soft dress of orange, yellow and magenta chiffon over my head.

It is sheer, but not see through and feels like a delicious kiss against my skin, which is still damp from my walk through the clouds.

He nods approval, "The colors of the sun suit you," he says "They match your spirit".

He continues, "Your mother is waiting on the other side, it is time for you to go to her. She has gifts for you as well."

He places his hand on my back just behind my heart as I turn to go. I can feel the heat of his palm ever so slightly burn my skin as if to mark me as his. His large square hand-print is now forever on my back as a birthmark, a brand that will bind me to him.

"Remember, I am with you always. Speak to me whenever you wish. The song in your heart matches mine. I will always hear you and answer."

I turn back to hug him farewell but he has already faded into the mist. So, I do as I have been told and head to the other side of the mountain where my mother the Goddess is waiting.

I feel her before I see her. Suddenly I round a bend in the path and she stands before me, her arms open as before.

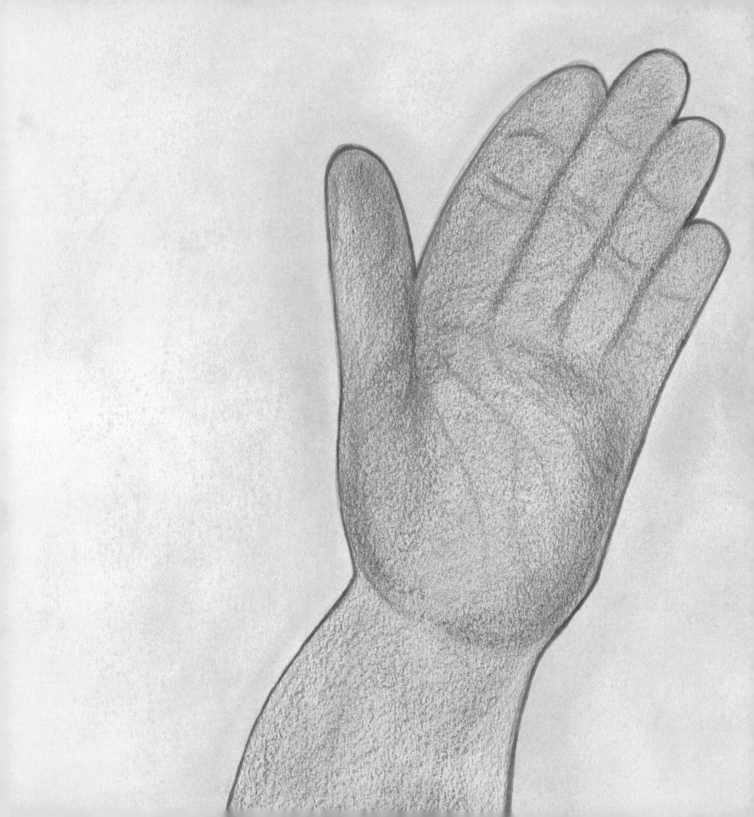

She is pure beauty, a rainbow light. Her melodic voice is like a harp and wind chimes.

She holds a velvet pouch in one hand and a tool belt in the other. I gaze in curiosity. Before I can ask she tells me. "This pouch holds your stone of truth."

I reach inside and feel a warm smooth stone as large as my hand.

"Hold it to your heart and pray" she says. "Pray, for the wisdom and truth that is yours".

She fastens the tool belt around me saying "These are the tools of your life. Your life is creative, your life is art and art is your life. It is where your spirit lives."

The belt is heavy, laden with paintbrushes, pencils, pastels, and collage materials. It is a magic bag. It does not look large enough to carry all that it does. It reminds me of the magic satchel carried by the nanny in the story "Mary Poppins." It does not look very big but when you reach inside, an endless supply of items present themselves.

The belt feels good on my hips, strong and true as though it had always been there, as much a part of me, as my own arm.

She takes my stone of truth from the bag, places it between my hands and folds my fingers around it as you would in prayer.

"Now," she says, "The last of your journey for today."

"You must travel to the Valley of Hopes and Dreams. Hold your stone of truth as you travel, with a prayer in your heart as you go."

"Quiet your mind and let your heart speak the prayers of your hopes and dreams. When you arrive in the valley, you will know that you are there. There are no signs, you will simply know."

I ask no questions, I kiss her in gratitude and turn to go. I am light and free and dance down the mountain with my hands folded around my stone. My heart flutters in silent prayer.

I arrive in the valley and am suddenly so tired, that I cannot keep my eyes open any longer.

I lay down in the fragrant meadow and sleep, my hands still curled around the stone, my tool belt still at my hips, flowers in my hair, and the gems of the Grandmothers at my neck.

I awake as the sun is setting. I lay on my back, with what I believe is my truth stone, on my belly. I move my hands to uncover it and there in the curve of my abdomen I discover that my stone has become a huge pearl. It is the size of a baseball. In awe I lift it to the sun; it is smooth and glossy, iridescent and creamy.

It vibrates with powerful energy and tinkles like it is filled with bells as it rolls in my palm.

It represents my wisdom, my confirmation that all is well. The message appears in my heart as..." I am the art, the art is me. I am the healer, the artist, the writer, the lover, the mother, the sister.

I am all of this and more. I am the goddess and the goddess is me.

I am Wonderment, no longer the wounded child. I am an adult and I have come home. I am whole."

"I have come home to all the gifts of the universe. My path is abundant. Joy and wisdom are mine," and I claim them.

CHAPTER 4

Day 3 Dark History Bright Future

Day 3

The Cave of the Ancestors

Fencepost Prince & Lily

Today the dawn is drizzly, soft spring rain is falling fresh and cool.

I notice there is the special smell that spring brings - the aroma of anticipation. I feel so ready to continue my journey. I tingle with excitement.

Yet, at the same time I feel just a hint of sadness because I know this is the final day. As I approach the place where I will meet my guide, I notice the first lilacs of spring are blooming near her door. I cannot stop myself from burying my nose in the damp, rich purple scent.

I smile as I inhale, and then burst out laughing as a childhood memory floods back. When I was about seven years old I visited my Great Aunt Hannah, I picked enough lilacs from her yard to fill her bathtub. I thought they were so lovely that I wanted her to have a lilac bath.

My mother was upset that I had stripped the bushes, but not my Aunt. She added water to the tub and had a lilac bath.

I can feel my great Aunt with me and I think today is going to be a very special day.

Today we begin at the lowest point of the island. I travel the edge of the low side, heading to the point on the island directly opposite the Mountain of the Grandmothers.

I find myself in a kayak paddling the shallows between the rocks and the shore. As I

round the next bend I find myself at the mouth of a cave. It is too narrow for my kayak.

I feel drawn to explore it. I get out of the kayak and step lightly to the mouth of the cave. As I approach I notice the opening is exactly the shape of my body, if I stand with my arms at my sides, but slightly away from my body with my palms up.

I accept this for what it is. My history, my ancestors are here and I know that I am meant to enter.

I can feel the whispering before I hear it.

As I enter the cool darkness of the cave my prism heart fills with light and throws dancing rainbows before me to illuminate my path.

I hear the whispers now. They grow louder and more distinct behind me, as I turn to face the wall that the sounds come from. I notice the drawings on the walls of the cave.

The images and symbols indicate fires, war, dominance and violent abuse. I feel the screaming, the suffering and pain as if it is my own.

I see pictures of warriors invading the farmlands of my family.

The images continue as the wall of the cave curves forward. The next images depict slavery. I can smell the fires of burnt crops still smoldering. The rancid stench of blood and soot fills my nostrils.

The screaming fades into a deep, submissive moaning and babies crying.

I am anxious to be away and turn to make my way out. As I move along the opposite wall, the images are of better times. There are abundant fields, lush gardens, sweet hay and fresh cream. The next image is when the drought and the locusts come and destroy it all.

I feel the hunger, the heartbreak, the helplessness. The people drink alcohol to ease their pain and numb the hunger. They give it to the children to stop their crying, and the children are damaged. The entire village is deeply wounded.

Next there is a woman, and she is the healer, the shaman, the artist, the storyteller. She is the guardian of the history and she is also the breaker of the chain of suffering. She is courageous and powerful. Through her heart centered wisdom she breaks the chain of guilt, shame, suffering, slavery and hunger.

She breathes life into the hopes and dreams of her family. She is brave, yet vulnerable. She acknowledges the past and tells the stories. Yet, she believes in brighter days and creates a better future.

She is the wounded healer. She has pure faith in a power greater than her own. She is the storyteller, the Shaman, the healer, the artist.

I recognize her because she is me. She is my alter ego, my highest self, she is Wonderment.

I cry for the suffering and pain of my ancestors. But, I know that it is done. It cannot hurt me; I need not be a victim of the past. I will create a new story. The chain is broken.

Fencepost Prince & Lily

I leave the cave of pain behind and continue to the foothills of the dome of the island. This is known as, "the Belly of the Sleeping Goddess."

I can feel the island breathe, gently opening and closing like a bellows, her breath matches my own.

Here is where my questions, related to my earthly parents are answered. They were lost to me long ago; I was often more parent to them than they were to me. Something I resented, but now I understand that they were broken in their life, their earthly journey. Now having seen the stories of the ancestors I know why. I see their story, and understand that it need not become mine.

I see the kingdom and around the kingdom there is a fence.

The man, who was my earthly father, is now a fencepost in the Kingdom. He has become a student. He has much to learn, but he is willing and he is happy in his role as a fencepost. He is a humble and willing student. He is still very much in love with my earthly mother.

He keeps watch over her, she floating in a pond nearby. She is a flower on a lily pad, pale pink and delicately fragrant. She is resting and watching my father, her Fence Post Prince. She gazes at him with the same love she always had for him. She has forgiven his weakness and is proud that he is humble and willing to learn.

I am happy for them both, especially my birth mother, who was neglected, and emotionally broken again and again in her earthly journey. Yet, she always remained sweet, kind hearted and grateful.

She deserves this divine rest, this blessing.

I feel peaceful knowing they are together in the kingdom, and that they are happy.

I continue to journey on and I find myself suddenly exhausted- overwhelmed by sleep, unable to take another step.

This is much like the scene from "The Wizard of Oz", where the snow in the poppy field puts everyone instantly to sleep.

I lay down under a willow tree, the branches hanging around me like a veil. The ground is covered in fragrant and soft moss and welcomes me to rest.

I do not know how long I have slept but I awake and stretch lazily. I pull back the willow veil first with my left hand then and with my right.

I look up to find myself surrounded with eyes of love.

My little sister, Jennifer who had died years before in a tragic auto accident, stands before me singing "Color my World," in her angelic voice. Tears of joy slip from my eyes at the sight of her.

Next my late husband Bert, who was also taken from this life after a struggle with cancer years before, is beside me. He takes my right hand and lays it upon my heart, his hand remains on mine. I smile into the crystal blue of his Scandinavian eyes. His lips brush mine and I sigh as I breathe in the aroma of cedar wood and Amaris cologne that always was his. I feel profound comfort at the touch of his beard on my face and his powerful hand on mine.

He smiles gently as he says to me. "You have done well my love; you are a wonderful mother to our daughter. I am sorry I could not be there but I am watching over you both.

Do not worry; love will come for you again.

You will know him; you need not look for him. I will bring him when I know you are ready."

"He will love you well, as I did and always will. He will know who you are and will honor your spirit, with no vain attempt to control or change you"

He continued, "I have chosen for our daughter also, so have no fear for I have chosen wisely. She will have the partner, the children and the life she desires."

He lifts his hand from mine and steps away just enough to allow the others to move forward with the gifts they have brought to me.

My earthly Grandmother, with a "Peace Rose" from the plant I had gifted her years before, my Great Aunt, with a lovely lilac, of course and my earthly

Grandfather, with a basket of farm fresh eggs. He used to drive us to the country to buy them from the farmers he knew.

Archangels Michael and Gabriel lay gold coins at my feet, paint brushes and good thick paper in my hands. My Spirit Guides and my Animal Spirits- the lioness and the hawk, surround me now and I feel a deep sense of peace. There is no resistance to these loving spirits that bathe me in their healing light. I feel filled with white light and it vibrates to the drumbeat of my heart.

All the signs that I have held up for so many years, now fall away. Signs I had surrounded myself with to protect my spirit. Stop, Go away, That will not work, etc.

All the signs are now tossed into the volcano and devoured by her fire, along with my armor, the thick, heavy mantle of guilt and shame that I had worn so long, thinking I was protecting myself. They are now melted in the fire.

My heart is open, my spirit light. I feel as though I have lost 50 pounds. I now allow love and abundance to enter.

The "City of Pain" is gone from my back. There is truth and forgiveness in my heart. There is peace. A sense of peace so deep, so profound, that I cannot find words to express it.

There is just a deep knowing that all is well. My intuitive "knowing" is my best compass. The future is bright and wonderful things are coming my way. I need only to learn to receive them.

I close my eyes and when I open them again I am now back by the tidal pools. I see the whales swimming back and forth between the shoulder rocks of the island. Their powerful bodies are pushing any lingering vibrations from the "City of Pain", into the ocean away from the island, releasing her, releasing me.

I have traveled the island to return to myself. I have revisited my history and let it go. I reclaim myself as the daughter of the King and the Goddess.

I embrace the gifts and talents that have been bestowed on me.

The future is bright, the old story is gone. The new story is mine to write and the possibilities are infinite.

I am free and I have come home to my spirit.

Wonderment is my highest self, the best and brightest of me.

I am the art, and the art is in me. I am the wounded healer. I am love and light. I know where I came from, I know exactly who I am, and what I came here to do.

I am Wonderment, and so it is.

"Knowing others is wisdom, knowing yourself is Enlightenment"

~ Lao Tzu

Authors Notes:

This book should never be assumed to imply that a Lomi-Lomi session will provide this kind of profound journey. This is simply my personal experience and I was ready to receive it.

After discovering my gift for whimsical art, I have continued my experimentation with art, using it as a platform to express my emotions. I have always thought in pictures- now I know why. I enjoy many mediums. I am self -taught, except for a brief figure drawing & oil painting class.

I feel divinely connected to my spirit. I am continuing to learn to use my own intuition and spiritual connection to help others.

Wonderful things are coming my way. I listen closely to my higher power and my intuition. I have no fear -only pure deep faith, in my ability to create my life.

Whatever path you choose to take to get there, I hope that this story will encourage you to stay connected to your own spirit and to embrace your own gifts.

For me, my daily meditation and my yoga practice help me to remain grounded, centered and true to myself.

My heart is open and I savor the anticipation of the wonderful future before me. I Am, after all, the artist and I will create a life of love, healing, creativity and storytelling.

Notes

My Goddess Mother is my universal "Higher Spirit" Mother
My Father the King is my universal "Higher Spirit" Father
My Lioness Mother represents my spirit animal the Lion
I was born on August 8 under the sign of Leo

The Grandmothers are my ancestral mothers back & back to the beginning of time

My biological parents were good people who tried

My father battled with alcoholism. My mother had been raised in an alcoholic family

She only had a seventh grade education.
She worked at service jobs her whole life and never knew her own self worth.
There was no social life for my parents.

Life was difficult for them and they both died young

My husband Bert was the love of my life. We lost him to cancer in 1997
when our daughter Zoë was just 4 years old.
He gave us enough love to last a lifetime.

My guide on this journey was

Cuky Choquette Harvey, Lomi-Lomi Master and Hawaiian Healing Arts Specialist

Resources & Recommended Reading

Cuky Choquette Harvey ~ Hawaiian Healing Arts Specialist

Dr. Michael Platt M.D. ~ "The Miracle of Bio Identical Hormones"

Dr. Gregory Pippert M.D. https://tcintmed.com/dr-greg-pippert/

Printed in the United States
by Baker & Taylor Publisher Services